Anonymous

Canadian Catholic Readers

First Reader - Part 1

Anonymous

Canadian Catholic Readers
First Reader - Part 1

ISBN/EAN: 9783337192709

Printed in Europe, USA, Canada, Australia, Japan

Cover: Foto ©Lupo / pixelio.de

More available books at **www.hansebooks.com**

Canadian Catholic

FIRST READER.

PART. I.

APPROVED BY THE EDUCATION DEPARTMENT FOR USE IN THE ROMAN CATHOLIC SEPARATE SCHOOLS OF ONTARIO.

Entered according to Act of the Parliament of Canada, in the year one thousand eight hundred and ninety-nine, by THE COPP, CLARK COMPANY, LIMITED, Toronto, in the Office of the Minister of Agriculture.

TORONTO:

THE COPP, CLARK COMPANY, LIMITED.

THE MADONNA.

PREFACE.

In this book an attempt is made to teach elementary reading by the phonic method, with as little help from the word method as is consistent with the preservation of a literary character for the lessons.

In the first six lessons are presented all the consonants (except z), in combination with the short sounds of the vowels. These lessons are in two forms—Script and Roman—so that the pupil may become familiar with the letters in both forms.

All the lessons in this book are based on the short sounds of the vowels. Lessons VIII-XII give these sounds with, in almost all cases, a single consonant preceding and succeeding the short vowel.

In Lesson XIII are introduced, formally, double consonants, and two consonants preceding or succeeding the short vowel.

Lessons XV-XXII give a review of the short vowels and the consonants in new combinations.

Lessons XXIV-XXVIII introduce words where one sound is represented by two pictures or letters.

Lessons XXX-XXXIV give a final review of short vowels with two consonants preceding or succeeding, or preceding and succeeding.

(3)

Lessons VII and XXIII are formal religious lessons in which most of the words are to be taught as wholes. One sentence of each of these lessons may be introduced at any time during the progress of the other lessons. This will give variety of work ; and will inculcate religious truths.

Lessons XIV and XXIX give short sentences for general review.

The detailed method of teaching these lessons, and a type " plan " for teaching the first lesson in each group of lessons will be found in the Teacher's Hand Book to accompany this series of Readers.

It may be stated here, however, that although the matter on pages 6 and 7 is called " Lesson I," there are, in reality, as many " lessons" as there are phrases or sentences. These phrases and sentences are in sequence. After the word *cat* has been taught, the succeeding words are selected, subject to two conditions : (1) the new word will present but *one new* picture (letter) ; and (2) the new word will be a regular step towards the early formation of a *sentence*. Thus : *cat, mat, sat, Sam, pat, hat, bat, rat, vat.*

Where a lesson departs slightly from the plan implied here for its group, the judicious teacher will easily deal with any difficulty which may, from this cause, arise in word recognition.

Aa	Bb	Cc	A a	B b	C c
Dd	Ee	Ff	D d	E e	F f
Gg	Hh	Ii	G g	H h	I i
Jj	Kk	Ll	J j	K k	L l
Mm	Nn	Oo	M m	N n	O o
Pp	Qq	Rr	P p	Q q	R r
Ss	Tt	Uu	S s	T t	U u
Vv	Ww	Xx	V v	W w	X x
Yy	Zz	&	Y y	Z z	&
1 2 3 4 5			1 2 3 4 5		
6 7 8 9 0			6 7 8 9 0		

a, short, in combination with c, t, m, s, f, p, h, b, r, and v.

cat   fat   hat   vat   mat
Sam   bat   sat   pat   rat

Words to be
taught as
wholes.

a
the
on
is
in
by

a cat   a mat
the cat   the mat

The cat on the mat
The cat sat on the
mat The fat cat sat
on the mat   Sam,
pat the cat. The hat
is by the mat The
bat is in the hat The
rat is by the vat

a, short, in combination with c, t, m, s, f, p, h, b, r, *and* v.

cat	fat	hat	vat	mat
Sam	bat	sat	pat	rat

Words to be taught as wholes.

a
the
on
is
in
by

a cat   a mat

the cat   the mat

The cat on the mat. The cat sat on the mat. The fat cat sat on the mat. Sam, pat the cat. The hat is by the mat. The bat is in the hat. The rat is by the vat.

fan　nag　man　fat　cap
gap　lag　cat　bag　lad
rat　Sam　sad　jam

Words to be taught as wholes.

not

do

has

Review:

—

a, the,

on, is,

in, by

The fan. The cap
The bag. The cap is
on the bag. The fan
is in the cap. Sam
is on the nag. The
nag is in the gap.
Sam is a lad. The
lad is not a sad man.
Nag, do not lag. The
rat has the jam. The
fat cat is not by the
rat.

a, short, with **n, g,** d, l, *and* j. *Review of consonants used in last lesson.*

fan	nag	man	fat	cap
gap	lag	cat	bag	lad
rat	Sam	sad	jam	

Words to be taught as wholes.

not
do
has

Review:

a, the,
on, is,
in, by

The fan. The cap. The bag. The cap is on the bag. The fan is in the cap. Sam is on the nag. The nag is in the gap. Sam is a lad. The lad is not a sad man. Nag, do not lag. The rat has the jam. The fat cat is not by the rat.

New pictures or letters, e and w; e, short. Review of a short and the consonants generally.

hen	men	wet	bed
fed	set	peg	web
pet	net	red	get

Words to be taught as wholes.

—

It

from

The hen. Dan fed the hen. It is a pet hen. The men. The men set the net. The net is wet. The hat. The hat is on a peg. It is not a red hat. The peg is by the bed. The web is on the bed. Set Dan get the web from the bed.

New pictures or letters, e and w; e, short. Review of a short and the consonants generally.

hen	men	wet	bed
fed	set	peg	web
pet	net	red	get

Words to be taught as wholes.

It

from

The hen. Dan fed the hen. It is a pet hen. The men. The men set the net. The net is wet. The hat. The hat is on a peg. It is not a red hat. The peg is by the bed. The web is on the bed. Let Dan get the web from the bed.

New letters, i and k; i, short. Review of a and e short, and the consonants generally.

kid   lid   pig   wig   him
tin   big   gig   Tim
sip   hit   sit   did

Words to be taught as wholes.

—

nor

see

The kid. The tin pan. The pan is not big nor has it a lid. Do not hit the kid, let it sip from the pan. The pig. The pen. See the big fat pig. It is in the pen. On the pen is a net.

The gig. The man. See the man sit in the gig. The man has a wig. Tim met the man in the gig. Did Tim see the kid? Let him see the fat pig.

New letters, i and k; i, short. Review of a and e short, and the consonants generally.

kid	lid	pig	wig	him
tin	big	gig	Tim	
sip	hit	sit	did	

Words to be taught as wholes.

—

nor

see

The kid. The tin pan. The pan is not big nor has it a lid. Do not hit the kid, let it sip from the pan.

The pig. The pen. See the big fat pig. It is in the pen. On the pen is a net.

The gig. The man. See the man sit in the gig. The man has a wig. Tim met the man in the gig. Did Tim see the kid? Let him see the fat pig.

New letters, o and x; o, short. Review of a, e and i short, and the consonants generally.

dog log rod fox Tom
top cob jog not
box Bob hot got

Words to be taught as wholes.

—

and
of
so
but
oh
with

The dog. The top. Tom has a big dog and a top The top is on the lid of a box; and the box is on a log.

The cob. Bob has the cob in a gig. It is so hot, the cob can but jog. Oh! Bob do not hit the cob with a rod.

The fox. The hen. Do not let the fox get the hen. Ben got the dog; and the fox ran to the den.

New letters, o and x; o, short. Review of a, e and i short, and the consonants generally.

dog	log	rod	fox	Tom
top	cob	jog	not	
box	Bob	hot	got	

Words to be taught as wholes.

and
of
so
but
oh
with

The dog. The top. Tom has a big dog and a top. The top is on the lid of a box; and the box is on a log.

The cob. Bob has the cob in a gig. It is so hot, the cob can but jog. Oh! Bob do not hit the cob with a rod.

The fox. The hen. Do not let the fox get the hen. Ben got the dog; and the fox ran to the den.

*New letters, **u** and **y**; **u**, short. Review of **a**, **e**, **i**, **o**, and the consonants generally.*

gun yet fun sup rug tug
sun but bun bud hum
up hut mug tub pup

Words to be taught as wholes.

—
will
he
have
some
she

A gun. Tom has a gun. The sun is not up yet; but Tom will get his gun from the hut; and he and the dog will have some fun.

A bun A mug. Mab has a bun and a mug. She can sup from the mug. She has a bud in her lap.

The top. The tub. The rug. The top is on the tub; and the tub is on the rug. The top can hum See the pup tug at the rug.

New letters, u and y; u, short. Review of a, e, i, o, and the consonants generally.

gun	yet	fun	sup	rug	tug
sun	but	bun	bud	hum	
up	hut	mug	tub	pup	

Words to be taught as wholes.

—

will

he

have

some

she

A gun. Tom has a gun. The sun is not up yet; but Tom will get his gun from the hut; and he and the dog will have some fun.

A bun. A mug. Mab has a bun and a mug. She can sup from the mug. She has a bud in her lap.

The top. The tub. The rug. The top is on the tub; and the tub is on the rug. The top can hum. See the pup tug at the rug.

Words taught as wholes; review of words already learned, all combined in sentences.

Review.

God	Him	cross	let	sun	His
sins	see	man	us	men	

Teach as wholes.

made all died loves each sky love
we oh day trees son ill pray

God made the sun, the sky and the trees. He made man; He made all we can see. God made us to love Him and to do His will. The son of God was made man for love of us. He died on the cross for the sins of men. God sees all we do. Then let us do no ill. He sees me and loves me. Oh! let us love God and pray to Him each day.

a short, with new combinations.

Rab	cab	wag	mad
pan	sap	tan	bad
nap	rap	gag	tap
Fan	lad	Tab	tag
ham	dam	Nan	

Words to be taught as wholes.

—

then
tree
in-to
light
I
them

Rab is not a bad lad. He put the rug in the cab and had the nag run for Tom. He then fed Tab, and let her have a nap on the box.

Tom is a wag, but he must not rap on the box. He

put the tag on the dog.   The dog is not mad and is not to have a gag.

Dan and Sam got some ham from the van ; and put it in the pan.

The man will tap the tree by the dam ; and the sap will run in-to the tub.   Fan and Nan sip the sap. The sun will not tan them.

—   —

The map and the pad are in the box.

The cat will lap up the milk.

Light the gas.

The cap is in rags.

I am not a man.

e short, with new combinations.

Ned	beg	hen	pet
bed	keg	men	vex
fed	leg	ten	
led	hem	met	

Words to be taught as wholes.

———

his

when

they

Ned did not hit the nag on the leg, but led it to the hut. He met the men. Dan, beg of him to get his cap, but do not vex him. The keg is at the hut. Fan will hem the top of the bag.

Ned and Dan go to bed at ten, when they have fed the nag and the pet hen.

i short, with new combinations.

fig	Did	Bid	rip	rim
rib	nip	mit	pin	lip
hid	bit	fit	dip	

Word to be taught as a whole.

No

Ned has a fig. The dog has a rib. Ned hid the rib, but the dog got it. Did the dog nip a bit from the rib? Bid Ned put his mit on and see if it will fit him. He will not rip it. Is the pin in his mit? No, it is in his cap. Mab will dip the cup in the tub and put the rim to her lip.

o̐ short, with new combinations.

Bob	Nod	dog	mop	job	rod
fog	top	rob	sod	hog	
lot	hod	bog	lop	ox	

Word to be taught as a whole.	Bob will wash the gig with the mop. ˙See him dip it in the tub. Nod to him. His dog is with him. He has a job in the lot to cut sod and put it in the hod for the man.
—	
wash	

A nest is in the top of the tree. Bob will not rob it. He will lop a rod from the tree. The rod is for the hog and the ox. They are in the bog and the fog hid them.

u short, with other combinations.

dug   rub   gum   pug   cub
nut   mud   cut   put

Words to be taught as wholes.

fall

find

Ben dug a pit.   In the pit is mud; and he let his cap fall in.   He did not rub the mud from his cap, but put it on.   He will get gum and a nut from the tree; and will cut a rod.

He has a pug and a cub. He hit the cub with a nut and it ran at the pug.   Ben hid his cap and the nut un-der a log and then set the pug to find them.

ck, ff, gg, ll, ss, *and two consonants preceding and succeeding a short vowel.*

back	duck's	dull	wind	pink
Jack	off	glass	barn	soft
sack	puff	grass	smart	pond
band	egg	Bess	help	drop
neck	eggs	a-cross	nest	corn
Dick	bell	glad	rest	hurt
thick	fill	bank	milk	must
lock	mill	hard	duck	doll

Words to be taught as wholes.

—

go
There
like
work
are

Jack will fill the sack from the bin in the barn. In the bin is corn. He will then put the sack a-cross the back of the nag; and the nag will go to the mill.

Dick and Bess sit on the bank at the mill. There is grass on the bank. They like to rest in the soft grass. They do not work so hard as Ned. Dick has an egg. It is a hen's egg. Bess has her wax doll. They are not dull or sad ; they are glad.

The cat has on its neck a pink band with a bell. The bell can-not drop off. Bess put on the band and the bell. The cat must not get the egg. It will sup milk un-til it is fat. It has thick fur.

Dick will lock the mill ; and will not hurt the duck on the pond. He got six eggs from the duck's nest. The eggs of the hen are not so big.

There is not a puff of wind. The pond is like glass.

The cat purrs.   The dog barks.

Snap is a black dog.   He can hunt the fox.   The fox runs fast.

The corn is put in bags and sacks.

The kid crops the grass.

Ann lost her pen.

He struck the drum.

I can see the clock.   It has hands. It struck six.

Ben spins the top.

The flag is on the flag-staff.

He went on deck.   We had frost.

Do not sit up af-ter ten o'clock.

Dan is best in his class.   The mas-ter helps him.

Let us bless the Lord, and trust in Him.   He will help us, and will not cast us off.

Help me, God.   God grant it.

He sat on a log at the end of the hut.

It is not dark.   See the stars.

Pick up the pin.   Pack the trunk.

Nell has a rib-bon on her neck.

I have a fig in my left hand.   I am
   fond of figs.

The rob-in sits in the tree.

Tom can jump a-cross the log.   He
   hurt his leg, but it is bet-ter.

Send for the par-cel.

He is a just man.   Man is but dust.

I will not of-fend God by sin.

Next morn-ing he went to the hills.

Do not climb up the lad-der.

The lamp is on the box.

The frog will hop, hop, hop.

Go ten steps and then stop.

El-len has a pink dress and a silk cap.

Stand on the mat.

Cut the top off the twig.

The yard is flat.

He plants corn in the gar-den.

b final, preceded by **a, e, i, o, u.**

Mab	nib	cob	sob	hut
Tab	rib	tub	logs	rub
web	Bob	Rob	cub	

Words to be taught as wholes.

—

Hear

oil

draw

come

Bob and Mab ran on the grass with Tab, and the cub. Mab fell. Hear her sob. Bob lost the nib of his pen. Tab has soft fur. Rub it.

Rob will not go to see the fun, for he must put oil on a bit of web, and oil the hub of the cart. He will then let the cob drink from the tub; and will put it in the cart to draw logs. The dog will get a rib when they come back.

LESSON XVI.

d final, preceded by a, e, i, o, u.

gad	bed	Ned	did	lid	rod
had	fed	red	hid	rid	sod
sad	led	bid	kid	hod	mud

Word to be taught as a whole.

—

made

Ned led the kid to the barn to be fed. He has a pan of milk. The pan has not a lid. He will not put the pan in the mud. The kid is a pet and has a red band on its neck. Ned made for it a bed of soft grass; but Tom had a gad or rod to hit the kid. This made Ned sad, so he bid Tom stop, and hid the rod un-der a sod to be rid of it. Ned can lift the hod.

g preceded by **a, e, i, o, u.**

bag	big	dug
lag	fig	jug
tag	bog	mug
beg	dog	pug
leg	fog	rug
peg	log	tug

Words to be . taught as wholes.

—

each
school
boy
which
sore
home
bread
tail

The men dug a pit in the bog. They put a big log a-cross the pit, and put a peg at each end.

Ned will step on the log.   He is a school-boy, and has a school bag on his back.   In his bag he has a fig and a nut.   With him is a pug dog which has on its neck a strap with a tag.   Ned has a sore leg; but he must not lag, for the fog is up.   At home, his sis-ter Ann has bread and a mug or jug of milk for him.   As Ned sips the milk the dog will tug at the bag and beg for bread; but Ned will tell the dog to sit still on the rug.

Rub the nag with the rag.
See the dog wag his tail.
The keg is not in the gig.
The fat pig is in the lot.
Let us jog on to the hut.
Dig up the sod.

dam jam hem rim gum sum
ham Sam brim Tom hum

Words to be taught as wholes.

water
wheel
been
where
lunch
while

See the big pond. The water of the pond turns the mill wheel. Sam and Nell sit on the dam to rest. They have been to school, where they did a hard sum. They see the water drip from the rim of the wheel; and they hear its hum. Tom will get gum from the tree. They have some bread, ham, and jam left from lunch at school. While they rest, Nell will hem the brim of her hat.

n *final, preceded by* **a, e, i, u.**

Dan	Ben	tin
Fan	den	bun
man	fen	fun
pan	hen	gun
tan	ten	run
van	bin	sun

Words to be taught as wholes.

two
shoot
shot
cow
fish

The man has two fat nags in the cart. He did not put them in the big van. He fed the nags with corn from the bin. He put the corn in a tin pan. The nags can run fast with the cart, but not with the van.

Dan and Ben will have some fun. Dan has a gun; Ben has a dog. A fox ran off with Dan's pet hen. Fan put bread and jam and ten nuts in a bag, and a bun for the dog. The den of the fox is in the fen. The sun is hot but it will not tan them. Dan will shoot the fox. List-en for the shot.

Her sis-ter is a nun.
The man ran to win.
Hear the din.
The dun cow is in the pen.
Pin the rib-bon on the hat.
The fin of the fish helps it to swim.

p *final, preceded by* a, i, o, u.

cap	dip	top
gap	hip	up
lap	lip	cup
rap	sip	pup
sap	lop	
tap	stop	

Words to be taught as wholes.

—

wood

through

that

head

nose

Tom and his pup are in the wood. Tom fell a-cross a log. He hurt his hip and cut his lip. He has a cap on, not a hat.

The men tap the tree to get sap.
Tom will dip the cup in the sap
and sip it. If the pup get at the
sap he will lap it up.

Sam did not put the stick a-cross
the gap. The nag can get through.
But Sam will lop a rod off the top
of the tree; and will then rap on
the stick or tap the nag on the
back, so that it will stop.

———

Tom is not a fop.
See the frog pop up its head.
Dan has a nap af-ter din-ner.
He was fed on pap.
The frost will nip the tip of his
nose.
Fred made a hop, step and jump.
Rip the band from the cap.

t final, preceded by a, e, i, o, u.

fat	pet	split	not
hat	set	pit	pot
mat	wet	sit	spot
get	bit	cot	but
let	fit	got	hut
net	hit	hot	put

Words to be taught as wholes.

—

lake
boys
their
chairs
take
out
fire
boil
eat

It is sum-mer. Fred and Jack have a tent at the lake. The tent is a gift to the boys from their papa. It is fit-ted up with a cot or bed, a blank-et, a big mat, two chairs and a lamp on a stand. If the sun is hot they sit in the tent or go in-to the hut. Spot, Fred's dog, is with them. He is a pet; and is so fat he can-not run. He fell in-to a pit; but Ned got him out. Jack did not hit Spot.

They fish with the rod from the bank, or they set the net. When they lift the net it is wet, and they put it on the grass to dry, af-ter they take out the fish.

They split a log and made a fire. On the fire is a pot, and in it they will put a bit of ham and let it boil un-til it is fit to eat. They can get nuts from the tree. Fred will put them in his hat.

x *final, preceded by* a, e, i, o.

ax   wax   fix   six   box

tax   vex   mix   ox   fox

Words to be taught as wholes.

—

nail

down

pays

Ben has six eggs in the box. He will mix sand with them to pack them. To fix the lid of the box, he will fas-ten it with wax, or nail it down with the ax. The pet fox must not get the eggs.

Ben's dog is not so big as the ox; but he pays a tax for the dog. Will this vex him? No.

Review such words as are made up of letters and sounds developed in preceding lessons; teach the others as wholes.

O God keep me safe this day and
   night.

Teach me to be good and kind.

May I love and serve Thee, my God.

Guide my young steps in Thy law.

All thy ways are sweet and true and
   right.

Lead me in Thy paths, and let me
not stray from Thee.

In life and death, young or old, I
wish to be Thy child.

Thou hast made me, I am Thine.

How can I love Thee if Thou help
me not?

My tongue shall praise Thee.

My lips shall sing Thy hymns.

I must pray to God when I rise at
morn, and when I go to rest at
night.

—————

We pray for those who are not
kind to us as well as for those who
love us.

God loves us, and He sent His
son who died for us on the Cross.

It is God's will that we should
work.

ch soft, initial and final.

chap	chips	much
chat	chop	rich
chid	chum	such

Words to be taught as wholes.

—

small

likes

How

fly

does

now

Ned is a small chap. He likes to chat with Ben, his chum. They will sit by the man, and see him chop the log. How the chips will fly. The man does such work as he is not rich. Ned lift-ed the ax and then let it fall on the rock so that it is now blunt. The man is much vex-ed, and chid Ned for this.

sh, *initial and final.*

sharp

Words to be taught as wholes.

marsh	wish	short	shut
dash	shed	ship	shot
rash	dish	shod	rush
sash	fish	shop	shun

This
stones
may
feet
toy
try
would
were
who
make

This is a shop. It is hot and the sash is up. That is a shed for the nag. The shed is shut. The nag is shod so that the sharp stones may not hurt his feet. He is fed with corn in a dish.

Tom has a gun. Frank has a short rod and a toy

ship. The rod is made of ash.
Tom will go to the shop for shot.
He and Frank will then dash off
to the lake where they will fish,
and Frank will try his toy ship.
They shun the marsh. I wish they
would not rush so fast. Boys must
not be rash.

At the lake was a log hut in
which Tom and Frank of-ten put
the rods and gun. But, in a big
storm, the hut fell with a crash.
The rods and gun were not in the
hut then, so the logs did not smash
them, nor crush the boys, who had
just run out.

Tom and Frank are nev-er harsh·
to the cat or the dog; and do not
lash the nag to make him go.

th, *as in* than *and* with; wh *combine with* a, e, i, y.

than	then	when	whit
that	this	whim	why
them	with	whip	

Words to be taught as wholes.

first

race

care

That is Tom's dog. It can run fast-er than the nag. When Tom had them run, the dog was first. This is a whim of Tom's. Mab went with Tom to see the race; but Dick did not go then. Why? He did not care a whit for it. Tom did not whip the nag.

th, *as in* thin, bath, *etc.*

| bath | path | thin | pith |
| lath | thick | think | moth |

Word to be taught as a whole.
—

too

The path runs by the pond. Sam and Bob sit un-der the tree, for the sun is hot. The tree has a thick trunk and big branch-es. See the moth flit past. Sam has cut off a small twig and will find the pith. Bob has a thin lath to make a mast for his ship. If it is too hot, Sam and Bob, will, I think, go into the pond for a bath.

ng final, preceded by **a, i, o, u.**

hang　sang　ring　dong　song　rung
rang　ding　sing　long　hung　sung

Words to be taught as wholes.

—

way

trees

This is a church.　See the cross.　Hear the bell ring— ding, dong ; ding, dong.　It is hung a long way up.　The man rang it.　It was rung for us. We shall go into the church and sing a song to God.　After we have sung, we shall thank Him and ask Him to bless us.　When we come out we may hear the birds sing in the trees if it is not too hot and the branch-es do not hang limp in the sun.

Review lesson.

He sprang a-cross the ditch and ran
  up the hill.

Lift the latch.

Let us sit on the bench.

Stretch the cord.

The log was burn-ed to ash-es.

On the Cross the Lamb is lift-ed.

Let us turn to the Lord.

When I have God I am rich.

Shall we go in to lunch.

The bell swings and rings.

Bind the par-cel with a string.

He dug a trench in the marsh.

We must quit the things of the world
  for God.

O, ever sin-less Vir-gin, ask thy Son
  to help us.

He is so strong he can lift the log.

The stick is ten inch-es long.

Did the cat catch the rat?   No.

The duck can swim.

Fetch me a bunch of twigs.

Put the clock on the box.

To the Cross I cling.

Mary, Bless-ed Mo-ther care for us,
     thy chil-dren.

God gives us all gifts.

Tom swam a-cross the river.

Did he drink the broth?

The black-smith shod the nag.

It is the fifth of March.

He is the third man on the list.

God is my strength.

Let us shun the things that make us
     bad.

We shall go to the church and as-sist
     at Mass.

The ship drift-ed on the sands.

Hand me a match from the match
  box.

It was his wish to go.

He is so much bet-ter he can sit up.

Which of the boys will help me?

The hen will hatch the eggs.

They sat un-der an arch in the church.

The men march-ed to camp.

Do not be harsh to the dog.

The sun will scorch the grass.

Tom and Dan will go to fish.   They
  will catch perch.

Hear the bird chirp.

The farm-er will churn the milk, and
  thresh the corn.

We have spring.

The fog is thick.

The fox ran in-to the bush.

He ran in the hun-dred yards dash.

a short, with two consonants before or after, or before and after.

flag	drag	land	Hark	fast
flat	stag	sand	lark	past
glad	raft	bank	farm	grass
plan	waft	rank	barn	drank
snap	camp	bark	yard	pranks
Brag	damp	dark	cart	

Words to be taught as wholes.

town
good
goes
says
fear
said
play-ed
our
soon
bye

Dan is on the bank by the lake. He and Tim like to camp out in the park when it is hot in town. We can see their tent with a flag on it.

There is Tim on a raft that the boys have made. Their dog Brag trots a-long on the sand. Hark! how he barks at the pet stag. But he will not snap at it, for Brag is a good dog. He is strong, too; and can drag Tim in a cart; but it makes him pant.

As Tim goes past on the raft, Dan says:—"Do not let the wind waft you a-way Tim." But Tim has no fear. He says:—"Oh, Dan, let us go to see Ned at the farm." "That is a good plan, Tim," said Dan. So, Tim makes the raft fast to a flat rock; and he and Dan go a-cross the land to the farm. In the rank grass by the path they see a lark on its nest.

Ned is in the barn-yard. How glad he is to see them. They

play-ed pranks in the barn and drank milk; and then Tim said:— " Dan, we must go back to our tent as it will soon be dark and damp." " Good bye, Ned." " Good bye, boys; come back soon."

———

Hear the band in the park.
They can see the mast of the ship.
Strip the bark from the tree.
The ant is a small in-sect.
There is a vast tract of land in the North-West.
Do not cast stones at the birds.
Fill the tank with water; and put the crab in-to it.
The boys clap their hands.
He has a good plan for his work.
It is a log of hard wood.
He was last in the race.

e short, with two consonants before or after, or before and after.

bled	held	end	bent	jerk	vest
fled	help	bend	lent	ferns	west
glen	belt	mend	rent	best	crest
bred	felt	send	sent	nest	
fret	melt	tend	tent	quest	
step	hemp	wend	went	rest	

Words to be taught as wholes.

one
day
we
all
new
coat
saw
my
low

One day we went to the glen to get some ferns. On the way the sun was so hot that we felt as if it would melt us; but we had a tent to rest in, when we got to the end of our trip. The tent was lent to us and was

Fred had on a new vest and his best belt; and had a cord of hemp to help fix the tent. He went to the crest of the hill to see a bird's nest; but did not step well, so he fell with a jerk and made a rent in his coat by the end of a bent branch. When he held up his hand we saw it was cut and had bled. We did not send him back, for he was well-bred and did not fret, but said:—"Mam-ma will mend the rent and will tend my hand." We sent him to see if the bird had fled, but it had not, so he was glad, and went on with the rest of us in our quest for ferns. When we left the bend of the glen, the sun was low in the west, so we had to wend our way back, and our hap-py day was at an end.

i short, with two consonants before or after, or before and after.

skip	slit	grin	swim	silk	firm
clip	spin	grip	gift	pink	rift
slid	brig	trim	lifts	think	mist
slip	crib	trip	gilt	sink	
flit	grim	string	milk	hint	

Words to be taught as wholes.

old
you
your
thread

When Will was a lad of six, he got as a gift a toy brig with a pink hull, and a gilt mast with a silk flag on it.

As his mam-ma tuck-ed him in his crib she let slip a hint that he was to get it. Next morn-ing he put

up his hand and felt on a shelf by
his crib. When he got the brig,
he jump-ed up and ran to his mam-
ma to thank her for it.

Af-ter he had his bread and milk,
his mam-ma said :—" The grass is
damp with the mist; but when the
sun lifts it, you may go to the pond
and send the brig on a trip."

It was not long till he set off.
When he got to the pond he said :—
" I do not want to put the brig in;
it may sink or flit off." A grim
old man that sat by said, with a
grin :—" Oh, it will not sink. It is
a trim craft and will swim as well
as a duck. I shall tack a string
to it, and you can grasp it with a
firm grip, then it can-not flit off."

At this, Will was glad, and
said :—" I thank you, sir."

He then slid it off the bank into the pond. A gust of wind sprang up and sent the brig off with a skip and a spin. Will was so glad, he felt he must clap his hands. As he did this he let the string slip from his grasp; and the wind sent the brig off. It struck on a rock, which dash-ed a rift in the hull, and cut a slit in the flag.

Will felt sad; but the man, with a long rod, got the brig back; and said:—" Do not fret, my lad. I think I can mend the rift; and your mam-ma can clip a bit off the end of the flag or stitch it with a thread of silk."

Will is now a lad of ten. He has his brig yet; but he nev-er lets it slip off as it did on the first trip.

o short, with two consonants before or after, or before and after.

clod	drop	ponds	thorn
plod	trot	cork	sort
flop	stop	fork	short
frog	soft	corn	lost
	pomp	horn	plots
	fond	morn-ing	crops

Words to be taught as wholes.

ride
could
blew
hay
fields
road
seen
valve
tire

Tom went out one morning for a short ride, on his wheel, of which he is so fond. He said he could go as fast as Dick's nag could trot. So he blew his horn and off they went with much pomp.

Tom said he felt as light as a cork. They went past frog ponds, crops of hay, grass plots, and fields of corn.

But when they got to the fork in the road, Tom ran a-cross a thorn and soon was seen to stop, flop o-ver a soft clod and drop into a sort of ditch. The valve of his tire was lost, so he had to plod home.

The blot makes a dark spot.

Tom trod on a nail.

The planks prop up the barn.

He gave his bond to the bank.

What sort of tree is this?

The dust will clog the wheels of
the clock. We must oil it.

LESSON XXXIV.

u short, with two consonants before or after, or before and after.

scum	snug	bump	hurt
club	drug	lump	turf
glum	drum	pump	turn
pluck	tuft	fund	dust
spun	hulk	hunt	just
stun-ned	sulk	punt	trust

Words to be taught as wholes.

years
lilies
clothes
soiled
very
stories
should
story
wrote
paper
dry
again
read

Jack is just ten years old; and his fa-ther has giv-en him a new drum. He is fond of it and taps it of-ten. But one day as he was march-ing along, he trip-ped on a big tuft of grass; and he fell with a bump on the hard turf. The fall made a lump on his head; but he did not sulk. He went to the pump and wash-ed off the mud and dust.

Jack and Ned have an old punt, and they of-ten go out on the lake to hunt for water lilies. One day, the punt, which is but an old hulk, turn-ed o-ver, and they be-gan to sink; but some boys who were on the bank swam out and pull-ed them in. Their clothes were wet, and soiled by the scum of the water; and they were very glum. But their mam-ma made them take a drug, to stop a chill: and they were soon in a snug bed.

Trust is their big dog. A bad

boy hurt him with a club and stun-
ned him.   Jack put him in an old
box and kept him there till he got
well.

Jack's fa-ther has a fund of fun-
ny stories, which the boys like to
hear.   One day he spun a yarn on
how boys should have pluck.   Jack
likes this story so well he wrote it
on paper with pen and ink.   He
went to dry the ink o-ver the lamp
and burn-ed part of the paper,
mak-ing a blur.   But Jack is to try
again, so that he can read the story
to the boys at school.

The man will churn the milk.
Rub the rust off the gun.
We must work for our bread.
The cam-el has a hump on its back.

www.ingramcontent.com/pod-product-compliance
Lightning Source LLC
Chambersburg PA
CBHW021522090426
42739CB00007B/737